DRINKERS IQ TEST

Approved by D.E.N.S.A.

TAKE THAT BOOKS

Take That Books is an imprint of
Take That Ltd.
P.O.Box 200
Harrogate
HG1 4XB

ISBN 1-873668-40-6

Layout, cartoons and typesetting by
Impact Design, P.O.Box 200, Harrogate, HG1 4XB.

Printed and bound in Great Britain.

CONTENTS

TEST 1
DRINKING HABITS

The opening round. More a test of your social etiquette than of your cerebral abilities. How do you handle sticky situations?

TEST 2
DRINKING FACTS

What do you know about the drinking business? See if you are being fiddled or are on to a winner.

TEST 3
LATERAL DRINKING

Everything is not as it first seems with these devious lateral thinking questions. You'll have to be stone cold sober to get them all right.

TEST 4
GENERAL KNOWLEDGE

Your chance to show off your knowledge of trivial facts connected with the imbibition of alcohol.

TEST 5
DRINKING PROBLEMS

Last orders. A collection of puzzles for you to solve while you wait for your friends to arrive.

WHAT'S YOURS?

Check out your scores and see where you rate on the Drinker's IQ scale of intelligence.

TOILET BREAKS

A little light relief between tests. Drinking jokes to tell your friends while you argue over the answers or add up your scores.

1. Desirable Shape

Which of the following shapes of drinking vessel
do you prefer...?

A) Paper bag

B) Tea cup

C) Beer tap

D) Thimble

SCORES

Answer A = 1 point. You are a wino.

Answer B = 2 points. You are a housewife and can't find time to
go to the pub between cleaning the house... washing up... cooking
meals... nagging... and throwing out the gin bottles.

Answer C = 3 points. Although you are an impatient drinker,
you have all the right tendencies.

Answer D = 1 point. Either you aren't really a drinker, or you
are on 100% proof liquor. Both are bad for your health.

DRINKER'S   IQ TEST

2. Pub Quiz

What is your perception of a pub quiz....?

A)   Trying to remember who ordered what.

B)   A good way to supplement your income if you 'swat up' beforehand.

C)   A way of finding out whose round it is.

D)   You are not aware that pubs can talk let alone answer questions.

SCORES

Answer D = 2 points.   Clever, but who is asking the questions?

Answer C = 1 point.   Check carefully that it is not yours before asking.

Answer B = 3 points.   But be careful not to get banned.

Answer A = 1 point.   Why do barmen always ask such difficult questions?

DRINKER'S   IQ TEST

3. Poke in the Ribs

You feel a sharp pain in your left side just below the ribs. Which of the following is the most likely cause of this discomfort...?

A) You are stood too close to the dart board.

B) Your spouse has finally located you.

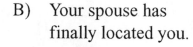

C) Your liver has decided enough is enough.

D) A dwarf wants to get to the bar.

SCORES

Answer A = 1 point. Try finding a new location.

Answer B = 2 points. At least you were there in the first place.

Answer C = 0 points. Should have been replaced years ago.

Answer D = 3 points. You are holding the good ground - don't move.

DRINKER'S IQ TEST

4. Bobby Dazzler

You are having a quiet drink in your local when
several burly policemen crash through the door.
Do you...?

A) Quickly draw a moustache
on your face and try to
look five years older.

B) Buy a round for everyone
in the pub to get rid of
the loot.

C) Rush to the toilets and
climb out of the window.

D) Pretend to be an undercover
policeman and bluff your
way out.

SCORES

Answer A = 2 points. You are showing very mature tendencies
in one so young.

Answer B = 3 points. What a generous person - mine's a pint.

Answer C = 1 point. Haven't you got the idea yet? You don't
leave your drink for anything. Besides, it will take weeks to
get the glass out of your backside.

Answer D = 3 points. Good initiative. Score an extra point if
you get the owner arrested and have your slate wiped clean.

5. First Orders

When you walk into your local, how long does it take you to get served...?

A) Your drink will already be sitting on the bar.

B) Up to five minutes.

C) Up to ten minutes.

D) It depends if you ordered Biryani or Madras.

SCORES

Answer A = 3 points. Just make sure it hasn't gone stale.

Answer B = 2 points. About average - perhaps you should try to make some more of an impact.

Answer C = 1 point. Change your local.

Answer D = 0 points. Idiot - you forgot to go for your pint on the way to the curry house.

DRINKER'S IQ TEST

6. Last Orders

Which of these would you pick up when last orders are called ?

A)

B)

C)

D)

SCORES

Answer A = 2 points. Your crotch is ruling your head.

Answer B = 0 points. There is nothing in your head.

Answer C = 1 point. Your stomach is ruling your head.

Answer D = 3 points. You are a discerning drinker, timing your run perfectly.

DRINKER'S IQ TEST

7. Odd Pint

Which is the odd one out?

A)

B)

C)

D)

E)

F)

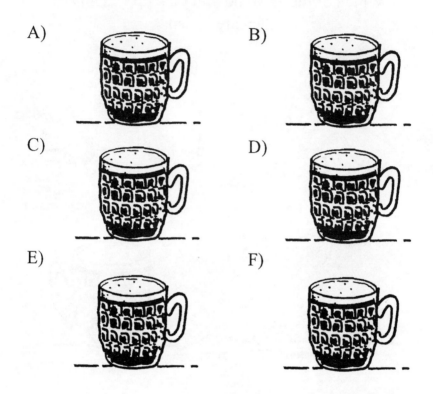

SCORES

Other Answers = 0 points.

across a similar situation in a bar.

problem, and find yourself a good solicitor in case you come

the others are all full pints. Practice your recognition of this

Answer C = 3 points. This is one drop short of a full measure -

---

DRINKER'S   IQ TEST

8. Best Leg Forward

You can feel a warm sensation down your left leg.
Have you...

A) Stood next to the fire?

B) Provided companion-
ship for a lonely dog?

C) Forgotten the way to
the toilets?

D) Spilt your drink?

SCORES

Answer A = 2 points. Seek a cooler spot.

Answer B = 1 point. Seek the owner of the dog.

Answer C = 1 point. Seek directions to the bogs.

Answer D = 0 Points. Seek medical attention.

DRINKER'S   IQ TEST

A man went to the doctor with a storming headache and nausea. The doctor made a thorough examination and proclaimed that he couldn't find anything wrong.
Smelling alcohol on the man's breath the doctor offered the explanation *"It must be the heavy drinking."*
"That's OK," said the man, *"I'll come back when you are sober."*

*I*t was two o'clock in the morning when the phone started ringing. The publican reached over and answered. It was John, one of his regulars.

"What time do you open in the morning?" came the slurred voice.

"Eleven o'clock" replied the publican and slammed the phone down in disbelief.

Fifteen minutes later the phone rang again.

"What time did you say you opened?" spluttered John.

"I said eleven o'clock, and I'm not going to let you in any earlier" replied the publican.

"I don't care about that," said John "I only want to know when I can get out of here."

A drunken motorist was stopped by the police whilst driving well over the speed limit. When asked, he explained he had drunk far too much to be able to drive, so he was hurrying home before he caused an accident.

*"D*octor, doctor, I feel like a glass of gin"
"Try taking a little tonic"

*"Will that be a pint of fighting beer
or a pint of singing beer?"*

"**D**on't have anything to eat on the way home after the amount of booze you've put away tonight," the barman warned Peter as he staggered to the door.

"Why not?" asked Peter.

"It will make you feel sick in the morning and give you one hell of a hangover!"

1. Taxing Matter

How much goes in excise duty for each £1.00 you spend on beer?

A) 8 pence

B) 20 pence

C) 25 pence

D) 67 pence

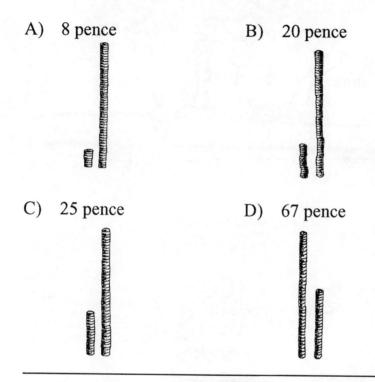

SCORES

Answer B = 3 points. And remember, you've already paid tax on the money you use to buy the pint!

Answer D = -1 point. You lose this point for being a friend of The Chancellor.

(The duty payable changes nearly every budget, but is charged at approximately £1.16/hectolitre for each degree Original Gravity over 1000°!!)

DRINKER'S   IQ TEST

2. Healthy Drinking

If a pint of beer is equal to two units and a glass of wine or a short is equal to one unit, what is the maximum recommended daily intake according to medical advice?

A)   3 units

B)   ½ unit

C)   2 units

D)   6 units

SCORES

Answer A = 3 points, if you are a man.

Answer B = 1 point.

Answer C = 3 points, if you are a lady.

Answer D = -1 point.

Low alcohol beers and lagers are ½ unit per pint, strong beers are 4 units per pint and sherry is 1 unit per 50ml glass.

DRINKER'S IQ TEST

3. Brain Drain

What is it that causes hangovers?

A) Dehydration of your body.

B) Too much fluid in your brain.

C) Impurities in your drinks.

D) A bad burger on the way home.

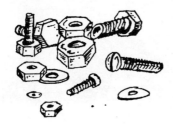

SCORES

Researchers agree that A, B & C contribute to hangovers.

Answer A = 3 points. Responsible for a general malaise.
Answer B = 3 points. Responsible for the headache.
Answer C = 3 points. Known as congeners - more than 100 have been identified.
Answer D = 0 points. A poor excuse !

DRINKER'S   IQ TEST

4. Crisp Crunch

If a bag of Salt & Vinegar crisps costs you 30p, and the bag contains 25g, which of the following would work out more expensive than your crisps per tonne?

A) Aluminium

B) Copper

C) Potatoes

D) Sugar

E) Nickel

F) Gas Oil

G) Live pigs

SCORES

Answer 'None' = 5 points.
All other answers = 0 points.
One tonne of these crisps would work out at £12,000.
Other prices are, roughly: Aluminium £833, Copper £1,050, Potatoes £50, Sugar £183, Nickel £4,400, Gas Oil £128, Live pigs £1,100.

---

5. Worldly Wisdom

What is the average number of pints drunk per head of population per year in these countries?
(Give your answer to the nearest pint)

A) Germany

B) Great Britain

C) Australia

D) Nigeria

E) Hungary

SCORES

Score 1 point for each correct answer.

Germany = 449
United Kingdom = 183
Australia = 197
Nigeria = 18
Hungary = 229

---

6. Heady Problem

What is the allowed 'head' within a pint of beer served in the UK?

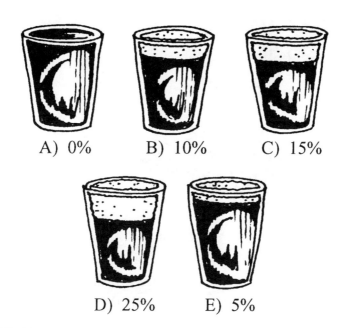

A) 0%   B) 10%   C) 15%

D) 25%   E) 5%

SCORES

Answer A = 3 points.

However, a recent case concluded that the head could be considered as part of the pint. Whilst it is no longer a legal requirement, you are within your rights to ask for the liquid to be topped up to the full measure.

---

7. Drink Drive

How much alcohol can you have in your blood and still be as good a driver as you are when fully sober?

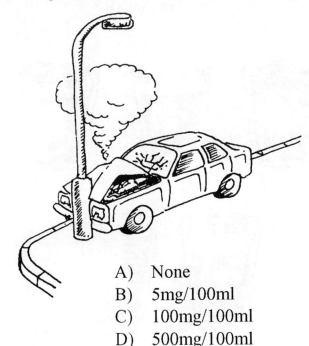

A) None
B) 5mg/100ml
C) 100mg/100ml
D) 500mg/100ml

SCORES

Answer A = 5 points. It is acknowledged that any amount of alcohol will slow down your reactions.

All other answers = - 1 point.

The legal maximum is 80mg in 100ml of blood or 107mg in 100ml of urine. Maximum penalties are six months in jail, a fine of £2,000 and more than 12 months disqualification from driving.

DRINKER'S   IQ TEST

8. Brauerei

How many different brewers are there in Germany...?

A) Less than 100
B) Less than 200
C) Less than 500
D) Over 1,000

SCORES

All other answers must drink a pint from each brewery.

West Germany alone.

Answer D = 3 points. There are more than 1,000 in the old

DRINKER'S   IQ TEST

Did *you* *hear* *about* *the* *man* *who* *fell* *into* *a* *very* *large* *vat* *of* *whisky?* *He* *drowned* *after* *three* *hours.* *Of* *course,* *it* *could* *have* *been* *quicker,* *but* *he* *kept* *getting* *out* *to* *go* *to* *the* *toilet.*

*J*ohn, the barman, asked a new customer why he was holding two pint glasses in front of his eyes. The customer peered straight at John through the glasses and explained that he was trying to make a spectacle of himself.

*T*wo sailors in a foreign land were on shore leave in a bar. When the two had reached a state of inebriation their sense of diplomacy left them and they went in search of trouble.

Stepping outside, the first thing they saw was a young native boy taking his donkey home from the market.

"Hey, boy," shouted one of the sailors, "Why have you got a rope around your brother's neck?". And both the sailors fell about in laughter.

Unamused, the little boy looked at the drunken sailors and replied "I'm trying to stop him running away to join the navy!"

A man left the bar and unwisely decided to drive home. On his way he was involved in an accident. Luckily nobody was hurt, but the police were quick to the scene. However, just as the police were about to take the man's details, there was a serious accident on the other side of the road.

The police rushed over to see if they could help. Sensing his chance, the man jumped in the car and drove home. When he got there, he put the car in the garage and rushed up to bed, certain that he had got away with his crime.

In the morning, though, he was awoken by the sound of knocking at his door. It was the police. "Good morning, sir," said one of the policemen, "could you please tell us where you have parked your car?"
"It's in the garage," replied the man with a smile.
"Could we have a look?"
"Certainly." And off they went into the garage.

But as they opened the door, the man's smile disappeared. There, in the garage, was a gleaming police car - with its lights still flashing!

1. Whole Hole

A man goes into his garden and digs a hole. The hole measures exactly 1.8 metres x 3.4 metres x 67 centimetres. He puts some of the earth into a wheelbarrow that can hold a third of a cubic meter, and carries it four hundred yards where he tips it out. This exercise takes several trips. How much earth, in cubic meters, is in the hole?

SCORES

ANSWER:
None = 3 points.
4.1 m³ = 1 point. For being able to calculate!
Any other answer = 0 points.
There is no earth in a hole.

---

2. Eggsactly

How many eggs does an average goose lay in one year?
Assume the goose weighs approximately four pounds.

SCORES

ANSWER:
None = 3 points.
Any other answer = 0 points.
It is the gander who lays the eggs, not the goose.

DRINKER'S   IQ TEST

3. Logic Crash

Flight AF 1037 was on a flight over some of the densest jungle in Africa. There were 38 passengers on board and four crew members of mixed nationality. At precisely 12:05 pm they ran into some turbulence.

Despite the best efforts of the pilot, the plane crashed. Only fifteen of the passengers and none of the crew survived the impact.

After only two days the wreckage was located. However, they discovered that the plane had crashed exactly on the border between the two countries.

This prompted a political row. Should the survivors be buried in the country from which the plane had taken off, or in the country to which it was heading?

SCORES

ANSWER:
Nowhere = 3 points.
You do not bury the survivors.
You can have 2 points if you belong to an international terrorist organisation and still insist on burying the survivors. However, you must then deduct 10 points for giving away your identity.

 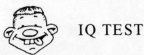

4. Ticket Trouble

One sunny afternoon you are driving a train from Little Herring to Greater Hogwash. To start with there are twenty four people on the train. At the first station, four people get on and six people get off. At the second station, ten get on and sixteen get off. At the third, only two people get on. At the fourth, five get off, three get on and then two of the people who got off get back on. At the fifth, ten people get on. The sixth station is Greater Hogwash. What is the name of the driver?

SCORES

---

5. Stomach This

An average man is five feet eleven inches tall. He weighs around twelve and a half stones. He is a social drinker and only goes out twice a week, never getting drunk. How many pints can this man drink on an empty stomach?

SCORES

ANSWER:
One pint = 1 point.
One sip, or less than a pint = 3 points.
Any other answer = 0 points.
After the first sip, or first pint if he drinks it in one go, his stomach is no longer empty.

---

6. Heavy Weight

Which is heavier:-

A) A tonne of concrete.

B) A tonne of iron.

C) A tonne of feathers.

D) A tonne of paper.

E) A tonne of Uranium.

SCORES

ANSWER:
None = 3 points.
They all weigh the same, one tonne!
If anyone argues along the lines of aggregation of gravitational acceleration or the displacement of air, they can have 2 points for choosing (E) Uranium. One of these points should then be removed because it was not stated on which planet the question was set.

---

7. Pick up a Penguin

How many penguins can a fully grown female polar bear eat in one 'sitting', following a spell of a week without food?

SCORES

ANSWER:

None = 3 points. *Polar bears live near the north pole and penguins live near the south pole.*

One point can be awarded to anyone who said any number if they were brought over in a frozen food container ship. But this must be removed unless they also stated the polar bear had a microwave to defrost the penguins. Anybody who made references to a brand of chocolate bar should have 2 points deducted for being silly.

8. High Jump

Do you think you can jump higher than....

A) A chair.

B) A dining table.

C) A washing line.

D) A house.

E) The Eiffel tower.

SCORES

ANSWER:

All of them = 3 points.

A washing line = 1 point.

None of the answers given can jump, so you should be able to jump higher than all of them.

Award yourself 1 point for the answer 'a washing line', for being a good high jumper even if you are thick!

*T*he rich boss of a brewery and a few of his henchmen were being shown around the works by one of the managers. The boss was known for his meanness, and everywhere he looked, he saw ways of saving money. This depressed the manager who felt sorry for his workers.

As they descended one of the difficult metal stairs, the boss slipped and fell into one of the huge vats.

Everyone rushed to help him. The first there was his right-hand man. "Quick, give me your hand," he said. But the boss just continued to thrash about, slowly sinking in the fluid.

Seeing a chance to become the favoured henchman, the number two pushed his way past. "Sir, give me your hand and I'll pull you out," he shouted. But the boss didn't seem to hear him.

The process continued with number three. "Before it's too late, give me your hand," he pleaded. No response.

Seeing that the boss was going to drown, the manager asked if he could be let through. Everybody made way and the manager leaned forward. "Here you go, take my hand and I'll pull you out." The boss suddenly looked relieved and grabbed the manager's hand, and struggled to safety.

As the boss recovered his breath, the right-hand man turned to the manager. "But why did he refuse our help and take yours?" he asked. "Oh, he wasn't refusing your help, "said the manager, "he just doesn't know the meaning of 'give' and only responds to 'take'."

A man and his son were having a few drinks in a bar. The son turned to his father and said, "Dad, how do you know when you are drunk?"

"That's easy, son," replied the father, "when those two lights on the ceiling appear to be on the floor - then you are drunk."

"But dad," retorted the son rather bemused, "there is only one light on the ceiling!"

A man walks into a bar and asks for two small beers. He drinks one and walks out. The next day he returns and asks for another two small beers. Again he drinks one and walks out. This is repeated every day for a week.

On the eighth day the barman cannot stand it any longer. "Why do you order two small beers," he demanded of the man, "why not take just one small beer or a large beer and leave half?"

"Oh," said the man, "the other beer is for my friend, because I don't like to drink alone." The barman sniggered and the man drank one of his beers then left.

The next day the man walked in and asked for one small beer. "What's the matter," said the barman thinking he was being clever, "has your friend died?" "No," replied the man, "my doctor says I have to give up drink because it is bad for me. This drink is for my friend." And he promptly walked out.

A steelworker always took a packed lunch to work. At break time he would sit down with his work mates and tuck into the food. He would then pull out a can of beer, open it, take one sip and throw it away. Every day for nearly a year, he did exactly the same thing. All his work mates looked at him as if he was a bit strange but said nothing.

One day, however, there was an apprentice who noticed the steelworker's actions. "Why do you always throw away your can of beer?" he asked.

"Because I don't like that brand" replied the worker.

"Then why don't you get your wife to pack a different brand in your lunchbox?" continued the apprentice.

"It's not that simple, son," said the worker, "I pack my own lunchbox."

1. Over the Moon

If you drop a pint in a pub situated on the Earth and it takes 0.45 seconds to hit the floor, how long would it take the same pint to hit the floor of a pub situated on the moon.

A)   1.52 seconds
B)   36.0 seconds
C)   1.11 seconds
D)   1.52 minutes
E)   It wouldn't

SCORES

Answer C = 3 points. Use the formula, s = ½.a.t²

Answer E = 1 point. OK, the question didn't say you were stood on the moon.

---

2. Strong Stuff

Which is acknowledged to be the strongest beer in the world based on Original Gravity ?

A) *Samichlaus* from Switzerland
B) *Roger & Out* from Sheffield
C) *Doomsday Ale* from Cornwall
D) *Itll Blowyeredorf* from Germany

SCORES

Answer A = 1 point. Samichlaus Dark is the strongest lager with an OG of 1123° and 14.9% abv.

Answer B = 2 points. This is the strongest by percentage alcohol by volume with 16.9% abv and an OG of 1125°.

Answer C = 3 points. This has an OG of 1143.5° and contains 15.9% abv.

All three will probably blow your head off!

DRINKER'S   IQ TEST

3. Matter of Mats

What is the correct name for beermat collectors?

A)   Sad People
B)   Matophiles
C)   Dripsologists
D)   Annoraks
E)   Tegestologists
F)   Labologists

SCORES

A labologist collects beer bottle labels.
Answer A = 1 point. *Socially, but not technically, correct.*
Answer E = 3 points.

---

4. Early Brewers

According to archaeologists, where are the world's first brewers supposed to have come from...?

A) Shaanxi, China
B) Sumatra, Indonesia
C) Sumeria, Iran
D) County Cork, Ireland
E) Bordeaux, France

SCORES

Answer C = 3 points. The Sumerians are known to have used barley to brew an ale from late 4,000BC.

Answer A = 2 points. Recent research indicates the ancient Chinese could have been brewing at the same time as the Sumerians.

---

5. Brand Names

Who brews the following brands of beer... ?

A) Head Cracker
B) Old Fart
C) Willie Warmer
D) Bishops Finger
E) Pig's Ear IPA

SCORES

E = Uley Brewery, Gloucester.
D = Shepherd Neame, Kent.
C = Crouch Vale Brewery, Essex.
B = Robinwood Brewers & Vinters, Yorkshire.
A = Woodforde's Norfolk Ales, Norfolk.
all five correct.
Score 1 point for each correct answer, plus 1 point if you get

---

DRINKER'S   IQ TEST

6. Who Said That?

Match the following quotations with the famous people who are alleged to have slurred them...

1) "I'm only a beer teetotaller, not a champagne teetotaller."

2) "O Beer! O Hodgson, Guinness, Allsopp, Bass! Names that should be on every infant's tongue!"

3) "I am falser than vows made in wine."

4) "Freedom and Whisky gang thegither!"

    A) William Shakespeare
    B) Robert Burns
    C) George Bernard Shaw
    D) C.S. Calverley

SCORES

Score 1 point for each correct answer, one point if you identified the script and one point if you got all four correct.

1 - C in *Candida* (1898), Act 1.

2 - D in *Beer*.

3 - A in *As You Like It*.

4 - B in *The Author's Earnest Cry and Prayer*.

DRINKER'S IQ TEST

7. Home Sweet Home

Where are the 'homes' of following drinks...?

A)   Trappist beer
B)   Gin
C)   Whisky
D)   Stout
E)   Champagne

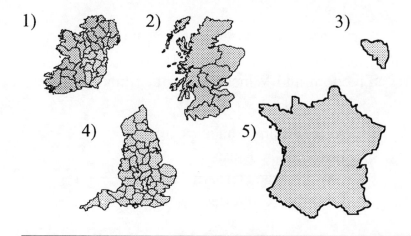

1)   2)   3)   4)   5)

SCORES

DRINKER'S   IQ TEST

8. Expensive Plonk

How much was paid for a bottle of
the world's most expensive wine?

A)   £10.50
B)   £105
C)   £1,050
D)   £10,500
E)   £105,000

SCORES

Answer E = 3 points. Paid for a bottle of 1787 Château Lafite claret, initialled by Thomas Jefferson. Take an extra 5 points if you knew the cork dried out in 1986 and ruined the wine!

*T*wo drunks, Fred and Bert, were having an argument about who was the best at everything. Finally Bert turned to his friend and pulled out a torch from his pocket. "OK, if you are so very clever," he said, "climb up this torchlight and touch the stars."

"Oh, no," said Fred, "I'm not stupid you know."

"Ah, you don't want to look a fool" jibed Bert.

"That's right," retorted Fred, "when I'm only half way up, you'll switch the torch off and I'll fall to the ground!"

*A*ll the ladies from a large office were holding their Christmas party. Everyone was having a great time and getting rather drunk. Everyone, that is, except Jane. She kept looking at her watch every five minutes.

"What are you waiting for?" asked her friend Samantha.

"I've got to rush off to the station," said Jane reaching for her coat."

"But this is the Christmas party," complained Samantha, "why don't you relax and have a good time. You can stay the night at my place?"

"I will," replied Jane, "I'm just timing it so I'll be late to the station and miss the last train!"

A persistent drunk walked into the doctor's surgery. The doctor looked up and his face sank. It was the fourth time Old Ted had been in that week.

With an expectant sigh, the doctor enquired about the latest ailment. After a pause and in a slurred voice, Old Ted told the doctor he had swallowed a horse and it was giving him a bad stomach.

Rolling his eyes in disbelief the doctor decided to teach Old Ted a lesson. So he gave him an injection to put him asleep for twenty minutes and called up a local farmer.

When Old Ted came round, there in the middle of the surgery was a dashing white horse.

"Everything's going to be alright now Old Ted," said the doctor, "I've operated on you and got the horse out of your stomach."

Old Ted looked very shocked, which pleased the doctor. "But, but, but!" stuttered Old Ted.

"Yes, what's wrong?" laughed the doctor.

"This horse is white," complained Old Ted, "The one I swallowed was brown!"

A man ran into a bar and pushed his way to the front. "Quick," he said to the barman, "give me a drink before the trouble starts." The barman being rather busy gave the man a drink and went on to serve his other customers.

Ten minutes later the man ordered another drink. "Quick," he said, "Give me another drink before the trouble starts." Still the barman was busy, so he gave the man drink and went to serve others.

This happened another two times. But on the fifth occasion the barman wasn't so busy. As he poured the man's drink he said "What do you mean 'before the trouble starts'? There isn't going to be any trouble in here."

"Yes, there is," said the man, "I haven't got any money!"

1. Drink Grid I

Find the missing number.

SCORES

Answer = 37.   Score 5 points.

2. Match the Drinks

A   B   C   D

1   2   3   4

SCORES

Answer:

A=4; B=1; C=2; D=3

Score 2 points. You may take 1 point if you had C=3 and D=2 if you assumed drink 3 was a softie and drink 2 was a half pint of gin!

3. Word Grid

Find the names of nine drinks hidden in the grid.

A	D	V	O	C	A	A	T
N	Y	O	C	I	D	E	O
X	D	D	R	M	G	I	N
S	N	K	K	E	A	D	I
T	A	A	I	A	G	N	C
O	R	A	N	G	E	A	O
U	B	G	O	E	R	R	L
T	R	E	T	T	I	B	U

SCORES

Brandy, Vodka, Tonic, & Lager.
You should have found: Advocaat, Gin, Orange, Bitter, Stout,
Score 2 points if you found all nine.

DRINKER'S   IQ TEST

4. Tee-Total

Add up the following...

Two G&T's

One mineral water

One pint of bitter

An orange juice

A vodka

and three kirs

? ? ?

SCORES

Score one point for any of these answers:
1) A cheque book job.
2) A man on a hen night.
3) Time to duck your round.

DRINKER'S   IQ TEST

5. Cross-Quiz

Find the word in the shaded boxes.
Clue: Congener contribution.

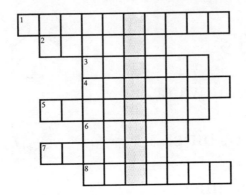

1. Blow into the bag (6,4).
2. Olde drinking vessel.
3. One shot, not married.
4. Same time every day.
5. Handy drinking spot (3,5).
6. "_____ again", morning after vow.
7. Bulk beer container
8. Female drink dispenser.

SCORES

6. Never, 7. Barrel, 8. Barmaid.
1. Breathtest, 2. Tankard, 3. Single, 4. Regular, 5. The Local,
Answer = 'Hangover' score 2 points.

---

6. Spot 11 Differences

SCORES

Score 2 points if you
located all 11 differences.

7. Lost Orders

Who will get the wine?

A

B

C

SCORES

Score 2 points if you identified the lady (B) as the wine drinker. The non-drinkers are A who has bought the crisps and C who has bought the pizza.

---

8. Drink Grid II

Find the missing number.

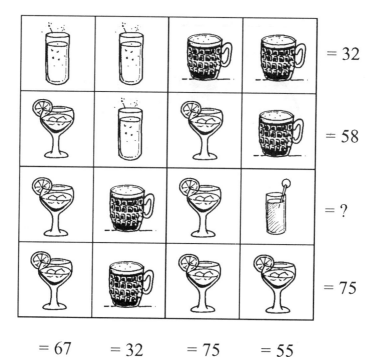

= 32

= 58

= ?

= 75

= 67   = 32   = 75   = 55

SCORES

Answer = 64.   Score 5 points.

= 21   = 10

= 4   = 12

DRINKER'S IQ TEST

*J*ohn and Tracy had just opened their little bar in a small
tourist town. Everything had been going fine, but this one
night a drunk had fallen asleep across the bar. He was there a
long time when John said he would throw him out into the
street. Tracy shook her head and told John to leave the man
where he was.

Half an hour later the drunk was still there. Again John went
to throw him out and Tracy stopped him.

On the third occasion John asked Tracy why she wouldn't let
him throw the drunk out. Was he a friend of Tracy's?

"No," said Tracy, "Every ten minutes he wakes up. I ask him
to pay his bill. He pays it and then goes back to sleep!"

What's Yours?

(Scores & Results)

TEST 1 - DRINKING HABITS

Over 24   What a good score. Are you sure you've added-up correctly?

15 - 24   What you don't know about drinking isn't worth knowing. You can hold your own while drinking in anybody's company and in any country of the world. That's just as well, because if you held anybody else's you'd be arrested. The air must reek of bullshit wherever you go.

5 - 15   You are getting there. A little more practice is all you need. Try having your liver removed and getting a divorce so you can spend more time on your hobby.

Under 5   Pathetic. Are you sure you are over 18?

TEST 2 - DRINKING FACTS

Over 30   Another good score. A bit suspicious don't you think? Check you're scores again.

15 - 30   Yawn. What a sensible bastard. Have you ever been to a party in your life? You must spend all your time reading bottle labels or interviewing publicans. Why don't you get a job with Customs & Excise?

5 - 15   A good balance of factual knowledge and complete ignorance. You can probably drink just enough and know when to stop. Get a life.

Under 5   How much did the lobotomy cost?

TEST 3 - LATERAL DRINKING

Over 24   Stop cheating.

15 - 24   A born lateral thinker. If anybody tries to trick you, you'll spot it miles away. The next problem you have to solve - is your paranoia.

| 5 - 15 | Perhaps you've heard a few of them before, or perhaps your friends gave you a few clues. Try reading the Maastricht Treaty to improve your lateral thinking abilities. |
| Under 5 | Oh dear! If it's not 'black and white', you've got a problem haven't you. You probably even believe everything you read in the tabloids. |

TEST 4 - GENERAL KNOWLEDGE

Over 41	This is your final warning - stop cheating.
20 - 41	You must bore the pants off so many people it's unreal. Your idea of a 'great party' will be a couple of G&T's followed by a game of "triv". How is the train number collection coming along?
5 - 20	So you paid some attention at school - what do you want, a medal? The only factor preventing you getting a better score is the fact that they don't serve booze in libraries.
Under 5	Thicko.

TEST 5 - DRINKING PROBLEMS

Over 21	You're banned for life.
15 - 21	The sort of person who completes the 'Times' crossword in the corner of a pub. Probably not the greatest conversationalist in the world. Never mind, it kills the time.
5 - 15	You aren't a true problem solver. The only time you use your brain in this manner is on the first three pages of the problem book you bought at Gatwick Airport on the way to Spain. Stick to making sure your change is correct.
Under 5	Can you lend me £10 and I'll buy you a pint to pay you back?

MORE HUMOUR TITLES...

The Ancient Art of Farting by Dr. C.Huff

Ever since time began, man (not woman) has farted. Does this ability lie behind many of the so far unexplained mysteries of history ? You Bet - because Dr. C.Huff's research shows conclusively there's something rotten about history taught in schools. If you do most of your reading on the throne, then this book is your ideal companion. Sit back and fart yourself silly as you split your sides laughing! *£3.99*

The Hangover Handbook & Boozer's Bible
(in the shape of a beercan)

Ever groaned, burped and cursed the morning after, as Vesuvius erupted in your stomach, a bass drummer thumped on your brain and a canary fouled its nest in your throat? Then you need these 100+ hangover remedies. There's an exclusive Hangover Ratings Chart, a Boozer's Calendar, a Hangover Clinic, and you can meet the Great Drunks of History, try the Boozer's Reading Chart, etc., etc. *£3.99*

The Elvis Spotter's Guide

Strange inconsistencies behind The King's 'death' have lead many fans to believe he is still alive. Now you can track him down with the help of a Priscilla Mask, an instant Elvis Ready Reckoner, 300 amazing Elvis Facts, a 'scoop' of pictures of The King taken since his 'death', cartoons of Elvis in his preferred professions, lists of his favourite meals, cars, girls, etc. And there is a reward of £2 million for the capture of The King. IN COLOUR. *£6.99*

The Beerlover's Bible & Homebar Handbook
(also in the shape of a beercan)

Do you love beer? Then this is the book you've been waiting for - a tantalising brew of fascinating facts to help you enjoy your favourite fluid all the more. Discover how to... serve beer for maximum enjoyment... brew your own beer... cook tasty recipes from beer soup to beer sweets... entertain with beer... But that's not all! With a listing of beers from all over the world, with flavours, colours and potency, you'll become a walking encyclopedia on beer. How better to win round after round by challenging your beer-loving mates in your local. *£3.99*

How to Get Rid of Your Boss

No matter how much you love your work, there is always one person who makes your professional life a misery - your boss. But all that can change. Find out, with the use of helpful diagrams and cartoons, how to get rid of this person that you despise. It's your chance to get your own back and really break free! *£3.99*

The Secret Lives of Teddy Bears
(with a FREE jointed Teddy Bear)

An explanation as to how those annoying little things in life really happen - who hides your keys, who alters your alarm clock and who causes taps to drip. There's also a Teddy Quiz... Bears on Film and Vinyl... Real Life Teddy Bear Facts... Teddy's Timetable... Teddies through History... and a lot more. *£3.99 - with free Teddy.*

The Bog Book
(in the shape of a toilet seat)
How much time do you spend in the bog every day? Are you letting valuable time go to waste? Not any longer! Now you can spend every second to your advantage. The Bog Book is packed with enough of the funny, the weird and the wonderful to drive you POTTY. Fill your brain while you empty your bowels... *£3.99*

101 Uses for Granny
"I don't want to be a burden," says Granny. Well, now she won't be. With 101 good uses, you'll wonder how you ever got by before. You can use your Granny to... Warn other motorists of your long load... Slow down incoming jets... Mark the fact that you've climbed Everest... Welcome your visitors as a talking doormat... Hold your TV aerial in the best position... and if you are ever short of a Guy in November... *£3.99*

Fatus Gitosaurus & Friends
A spotter's guide to modern dinosaurs. Discover how to identify The Commutosaur (Layt Yetagenus)... The Secretarosaur (Ofis Receptus)... The Bratosaur (Pestus Konstantus)... and many others. Each dinosaur is catalogued along with its habitat, feeding patterns and social behaviour. Discover the favourite food of the Revosaurus (Moretea Vica)... Learn to identify the terrifying Bossodon (Slavedrivus Rex)... and avoid the Blottotops (Dino Nonerectus) when stumbling into your local pub. *£3.99*

A Wunch of Bankers
Do you HATE BANKS? Then you need this collection of stories aimed directly at the crotch of your bank manager. A Wunch of Bankers mixes cartoons and jokes about banks with real-life horror stories of the bare-faced money-grabbing tactics of banks. If you think you've been treated badly, read these stories!!!! *£3.99*

Please send me a copy of

I enclose a cheque/payment made payable to 'Take That Ltd'. **Postage is free within the U.K.** Please add £1 per title in other EEC countries and £3 elsewhere.

Name:_____

Address:_____

_____

_____

Postcode:_____

Please return to:
Take That Books, P.O.Box 200, Harrogate, HG1 4XB

If you would rather not damage your copy of *The Drinker's IQ Test*, please use plain paper and remember to include all the details listed below!